GIFTED
&
TALENTED®

*To develop
your child's gifts
and talents*

STORY STARTERS

My First Stories

By Diane Cuneo

Illustrated by Kerry Manwaring

Lowell House
Juvenile
Los Angeles

CONTEMPORARY BOOKS
Chicago

Requests for such permissions should be addressed to:

Lowell House Juvenile
2029 Century Park East, Suite 3290
Los Angeles, CA 90067

Lowell House books can be purchased at special discounts when ordered in bulk
for premiums and special sales. Contact Department VH at the above address.

Manufactured in the United States of America

ISBN: 1-56565-240-1

10 9 8 7 6 5 4 3 2 1

GIFTED AND TALENTED® STORY STARTERS: My First Stories will help develop your child's natural talents and gifts by providing story-telling and writing activities to enhance critical and creative thinking skills. These skills of logic and reasoning teach children **how to think**. They are precisely the skills emphasized by teachers of gifted and talented children. Here are some of the skills you will find:

- Deduction — the ability to reach a logical conclusion by interpreting clues

- Understanding Relationships — the ability to recognize how objects, shapes, and words are similar or dissimilar; to classify or categorize

- Sequencing — the ability to organize events, numbers; to recognize patterns

- Inference — the ability to reach logical conclusions from given or assumed evidence

- Creative Thinking — the ability to generate unique ideas; to compare and contrast the same elements in different situations; to present imaginative, numerous solutions to problems; to develop or expand on ideas, stories, or illustrations

The Fill-in-the-Blank Exercises at the beginning of this book will help your child gain confidence in the story-telling (and story-writing) process. The child has two choices: **a)** to select words from the appropriate word lists to drop into the blank spaces; **b)** to use other words or phrases of his or her own choosing to fill in the blanks.

Using the word lists expands the young child's concept of what makes a "good" story. With the word lists, the hero can be a girl or a boy, a duck, or even a kitchen appliance. It is recommended that the word lists be used first, and that you read the stories with your child again, after all the blanks have been filled in. Once the child feels comfortable with the creative freedom to tell his or her own stories, the Fill-in-the-Blank Exercises can be reused, with your child providing new words for the blanks.

To help your child grasp the "purpose" and "place" of certain words (like adjectives and nouns), read words to the child from the lists, then ask the child to make up his or her own words instead, words "like" the ones on the lists. Going over the exercises reinforces not only the function of language but its richness as well.

It is important not to be judgmental about your child's choices. The word lists reflect the variety of language, so that the child does not form too narrow or too rigid a concept of what is "properly" a hero or "properly" a descriptive word. A child who rejects a word list and chooses to describe a morning as "yellow" and the hero as "a doorknob" has a very interesting story in the works.

Next you will find Eye-Opening Descriptive Exercises, which will encourage your child to pay more attention to his or her environment. Through the use of questions, the activities will teach the child to mine his or her own experiences and observations for story ideas. Each exercise stresses the collection of facts for immediate use in an original story. Note-taking should be encouraged. Visual as well as verbal clues and cues are used. If the child makes a visual observation, call attention to it, and/or write it down for later use in the story.

Sight is the most well-developed observatory sense, but exercises in this section will focus on all five senses to help the child develop a rich and well-rounded ability to write descriptions. Please note that these are observation and description exercises, not writing exercises. It's okay to write down your child's responses for him or her, and to allow the child to concentrate only on observation. When the child answers a question, ask more questions to draw out even more detail.

After the child moves through the Fill-in-the-Blank Exercises and develops an "ear, eye, nose, taste, and touch" for telling a story through the Eye-Opening Descriptive Exercises, he or she will be ready for Write the Middle and Write the Ending Exercises. Here, stories are started for the child, and the child then has to provide either the middle or the end. To help your child through the middle exercises, remember that the middle of a story is a link that provides a logical chain of events from the beginning (provided) to the end (provided). So ask the child to read the ending out loud and imagine what could have happened to lead to such an end. To help your child through the ending exercises, ask him or her to imagine more than one way the story can conclude. The more children use their imaginations, the more they will move away from clichéd endings and into creative endings.

The final section contains Advanced Exercises. These provide little help in the creation and writing of each story. The child is given scenarios for stories, but unlike the earlier exercises, no portion of a story is provided. Please encourage your child to consider his or her initial effort as a first draft. Once he or she has completed an Advanced Exercise and some time has passed, ask the child to expand on the first attempt on another piece of paper. You will both be surprised at how effortlessly the second (and third) drafts become more complete, and even more interesting stories.

Participate with and read to your children. Help them with harder words. A child's imagination should not be limited only to those words he or she can read, since children understand the meaning of words even if they cannot read them. The same is true for those words they cannot write. If necessary, record your child's stories for him or her. Regardless of whether your child can write full, complete sentences, your child will gain much from this book. Exercising the imagination is what **GIFTED & TALENTED® STORY STARTERS** is all about.

Good luck, have fun, and remember: good writers read, so go to the library often with your child.

Complete the story by filling in the blanks. Match the numbers under the blank lines to the word lists across from them. Choose words from the lists to tell the story. You can even choose words of your own! Read the story out loud when you are finished.

A STRANGE MORNING

By _____

One _____ morning I woke up and found that I had
           1

been turned into a _____. I was very _____.
                     2   3

I had _____ all over my body. They were_____
        4   5

and _____. At home, my _____ gave me a
      5   6

_____ and told me to eat my cereal. But I wanted
   7

a _____ instead. At school, my _____ was
    8   9

_____, and I had to sit in a _____. Finally,
   10   11

they called a _____,
                 12

and I was soon back to being

myself. Everyone said,

" _____ " and I
      13

agreed with them!

The End

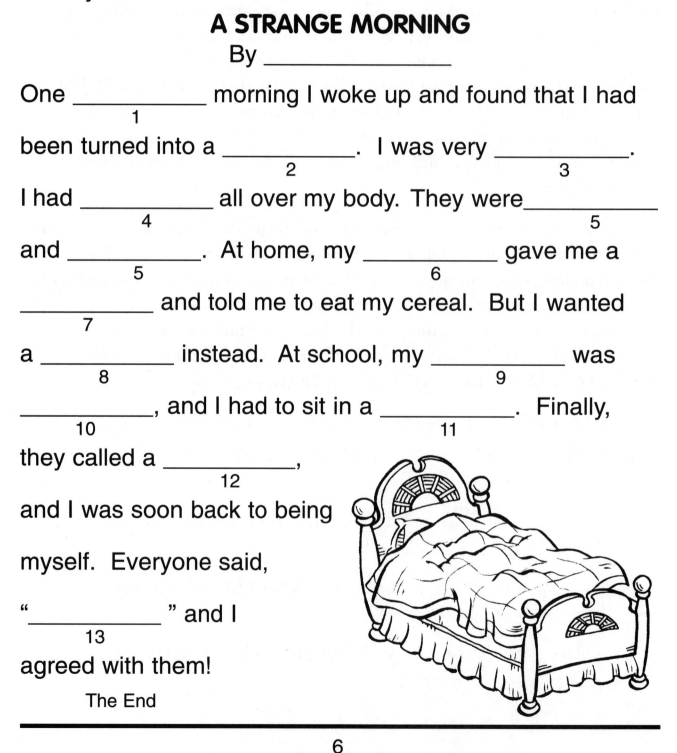

Word Lists

(1) bright, cloudy, dark, cold, messy, cool, breezy, strange

(2) bagel, butterfly, saxophone, monster, bug, baby, frog, toaster

(3) round, happy, green, shiny, sad, beautiful, scary, tiny, hot

(4) crumbs, tattoos, colors, buttons, scales, legs, spots, hairs

(5) funny, green, sticky, cool, weird, itchy, funny, gold, shiny, yellow

(6) mom, dog, dad, sister, brother, grandma, friend, aunt, fish

(7) bone, spoon, pat, rub, spanking, kiss, fork, scolding, hug

(8) fly, bottle, spider, cookie, flower, drink, boat, tree

(9) teacher, classmate, friend, principal, homework, book, desk

(10) shocked, amazed, surprised, scared, laughing, hard, too big, heavy

(11) box, locker, plant, pocket, drawer, chair, hat, closet, thimble

(12) doctor, janitor, veterinarian, scientist, magician, witch, nurse

(13) Wowzers! Time to eat! Finally! What a day! Jeepers! Let's dance!

Complete the stories by filling in the blanks. Use the word lists across from each story to help you. Draw a picture to go with each story in the space below it. Read the stories out loud when you are finished.

THE SECRET HIDING PLACE

By _____

One day I was _____ home when I saw a little
                    1

_____ running across the sidewalk. I followed it into
       2

a _____. It was _____ and _____.
       3   4   4

This _____ me, but I did not give up. There were
        5

_____ growing on the ceiling, and there were lots of
       6

_____ on the walls. Just then, a _____ jumped
       7   8

out and _____ me! "This is a secret hiding place for
           9

_____. Do you want to _____?" it said. I said,
     10   11

"_____," and then I went _____.
     12   13

The End

drawn by _____

Word Lists

(1) skipping, walking, dancing, crawling, hopping, running, rolling, wiggling

(2) rabbit, dinosaur, dog, troll, mouse, monster, spider, tiger

(3) hole, tunnel, boat, can, box, cave, nest, bush, tree, log

(4) dark, wet, high, skinny, empty, hollow, cold, deep, dirty, clean, smelly, pretty

(5) scared, tickled, surprised, fooled, bored, confused, delighted, angered

(6) pickles, dog bones, noses, flowers, cakes, dirty socks, branches

(7) lamps, fireflies, pictures, bugs, toys, sleds, webs, carrots, footprints

(8) waterbug, polar bear, kitten, bear, ghost, doll, duck, dinosaur, hermit

(9) hugged, yelled at, tickled, scared, tripped, kissed, stopped, stared at, laughed at

(10) first graders, second graders, big brothers, big sisters, spinach lovers, animals

(11) join, stay, leave, run, hide, tattle, dance, eat, giggle

(12) Yes, No, Maybe later, This is weird, I'd love to, Forget it, I have to go, Awesome

(13) home, away, inside, down, off, under, out

I FOUND A _____

By _____

One day in the middle of my _____ I found a

1

_____ that had _____ _____ and

2   3   4

_____ _____. I put it in my _____ and

3   4   5

ran to my friend's house. Later, we fed it _____ and

6

_____, and suddenly, it _____! I thought we

7   8

would get _____. So I put it _____ and sent it

9   10

to _____. I have not seen it since, which makes me

11

feel _____.

12

The End

drawn by _____

Word Lists

(1) backyard, forehead, shoe, playground, room, bed, sandwich, porch

(2) wicked witch, ladybug, wart, termite, superhero, plant, snake, space alien

(3) big, little, green, red, purple, six, one, fifteen, fat, bubbly, sharp, melted

(4) arms, legs, eyes, hair, pockets, antennae, fingers, toes, teeth, skin, knees

(5) pocket, wagon, bag, basket, bedsheet, sock, trash can, sister's purse, brother's pants

(6) cookies, paint, grass, sponges, chicken, broccoli, tin cans

(7) forks, hot dogs, french fries, pizza, hot peppers, staples, water, gum

(8) grew, shrank, talked, burped, growled, popped, wet, turned purple, cried

(9) in trouble, eaten, yelled at, a reward, messy, sick

(10) in the mail, in a box, in a rocket, on a bus, under the bed, in the toilet

(11) Hawaii, Santa Claus, my aunt, the zoo, the moon, my teacher

(12) good, happy, bad, funny, worried, scared, mad, silly

IF I WERE AN ANIMAL

By _____

Have you ever wished you were an animal? I have!

I would be a _____ and would _____ all day.
                        1   2

I would have _____ the color of _____. I would
                        3   4

live in a _____. On _____ nights, I would hide
                 5   6

in a _____. During the day, I would go to the
            7

_____ and make lots of _____. When people
       8   9

saw me coming, they would _____. I would eat
                                   10

_____ every day. When I was feeling _____,
       11   12

I would_____. Wouldn't that be _____?
            13   14

The End

drawn by _____

Word Lists

(1) tiger, snake, bear, lion, dog, cat, kangaroo, dragon, shark, whale

(2) sleep, eat, growl, run, swim, hop, fish, stomp, roll in mud, burp

(3) fur, eyes, skin, teeth, horns, breath, friends, scales, a tongue, toenails

(4) mud, spaghetti, slime, roses, bananas, the sky, fire, the sun, water, the ocean

(5) boat, milk carton, forest, jungle, cave, ocean, tunnel, house, tree

(6) dark, warm, creepy, black, cool, quiet, Saturday, moonlit, school

(7) blanket, cave, hole, basement, cage, locker, closet, pair of pants

(8) pool, supermarket, factory, mall, park, movies, library

(9) noise, pizzas, trouble, people happy, crafts, friends

(10) run, yell, clap, smile, take pictures, eat faster, giggle, cry

(11) cookies, bugs, potato chips, mud, vegetables, candy, jelly beans, ants

(12) tired, lucky, happy, sad, proud, silly, smart, hungry, playful, angry

(13) sleep, eat a bug, read, sing, cry, yell, hop, play cards, draw

(14) awesome, crazy, silly, cool, amazing, fun, ridiculous, terrific, wild, perfect

Here, you can rewrite a favorite fairy tale! After you finish, read the story again. Don't forget to give YOUR fairy tale a new title!

LITTLE _____ RIDING HOOD
By _____

Once upon a time there was a little_____ called Little
                                              1

_____ Riding Hood. One day, Little went to
     2

_____ house with a basket full of _____. "Be
     3   4

careful of the Big, Bad _____," Mother had said. On
                              5

the way, Little met Big. "I would like to _____ Little
                                                  6

_____ Riding Hood," thought Big. And away Big ran.
     2

When Little got to the house, Little saw Big in

disguise. "My, what big _____ you
                                7

have," Little said. "The better to _____
                                          8

you with, my dear," said Big. Then Big tore off the disguise

and _____ Little around the room. Little _____
        9   10

so loud, a _____ came in and _____ Big out
                11   12

the door. And Little _____ _____ ever after.
                            13   14

The End

Word Lists

(1) girl, duck, ballerina, pony, caboose, boy, dog, convertible, cyclops, Stegosaurus

(2) Red, Furry, Purple, Wrinkled, Green, Scaly, Pink, Goofy, Colorful, Speedy, Yellow

(3) Grandma's, the President's, the teacher's, Rabbit's, a friend's, Auntie's, a cousin's

(4) food, rocks, hamburgers, coloring books, pudding, mice, flowers, glop

(5) Wolf, Mouse, Toaster, Tyrannosaurus, Troll, Stop Sign, Kitty, Goldfish, Butterfly

(6) eat, tickle, hug, race, dance with, draw, quiz, play with, pinch, trick

(7) eyes, feet, sandwiches, ears, wheels, horns, hands, pencils, wings

(8) see, hear, tickle, wrestle, scare, trick, eat, hug, draw

(9) chased, danced, tickled, rolled, pulled, bounced, pushed

(10) screamed, roared, laughed, honked, barked, growled, tooted, cried, quacked

(11) woodcutter, waitress, gym teacher, crossing guard, tiger, guard dog, kangaroo

(12) chased, waltzed, shoved, carried, tossed, scared, bounced, threw, laughed

(13) lived, ate, bowled, shopped, danced, played, slept, shouted, galloped

(14) happily, slowly, sloppily, quickly, nicely, loudly, badly, prettily, sadly

Are you ready to try one on your own? Good! Read the story below. It is missing some important parts! Use your imagination to fill in the blanks and make up your OWN story. When you are finished, read your story again.

THE MYSTERIOUS NOTE

By _____

Paul and Kalie were eating a _____ in the _____ one day, when they heard a knock on the door. Outside the door, they found a note that told them to do something. There was food on the note. The note said:

_____

_____

_____

Paul and Kalie felt _____. Who left the note? They went outside and found a _____. It was _____ and _____. This was a clue! They kept walking. "Look!" said Paul. He _____ to the _____. There were footprints. "_____!" said Kalie. The footprints led to a _____ where they saw a _____ eating a _____. "Did you leave this note?" Paul and Kalie asked. "_____," said the _____. The mystery was _____!

The End

In the space below, draw a picture to go with your story. Think about what Paul and Kalie look like. Think about who — or what — left the note. Think about the neighborhood the children live in. Draw a picture using as much detail as possible.

drawn by _____

Look closely at the entire picture. Then answer the questions on the next page.

Your answers to these questions will help you write a story about the cat and the mouse. Write your answers on the lines.

What is the cat wearing? _____

How does the cat feel? _____

What is the mouse wearing? _____

How does the mouse feel? _____

Is the ship big or little? _____

Neat or messy? _____

What parts of the ship can't you see? _____

_____

What are the cat and mouse doing? _____

Are they friends? _____

Where are they coming from? _____

Where are they going? _____

Are they having an adventure? _____

What kind? _____

Who will win the checker game? _____

What is the cat's job? _____

What is the mouse's job? _____

Use your ideas from the last page to fill in the blanks of this story. After you fill in the blanks, keep writing. YOU decide what happens in the story!

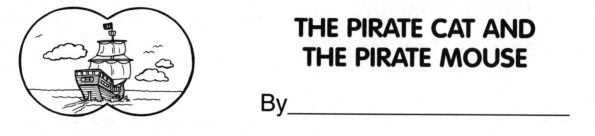

THE PIRATE CAT AND THE PIRATE MOUSE

By_____

The pirate cat and the pirate mouse were on a _____ ship. The ship was _____ and _____. The ship had _____ and a _____. The cat wore a _____ _____ _____, and the mouse had on a _____ _____ and _____. They both looked _____! They had been at sea for _____. They were feeling _____, and so they played checkers. _____ was winning. Where had they come from? Where were they going? Here is the rest of their story:

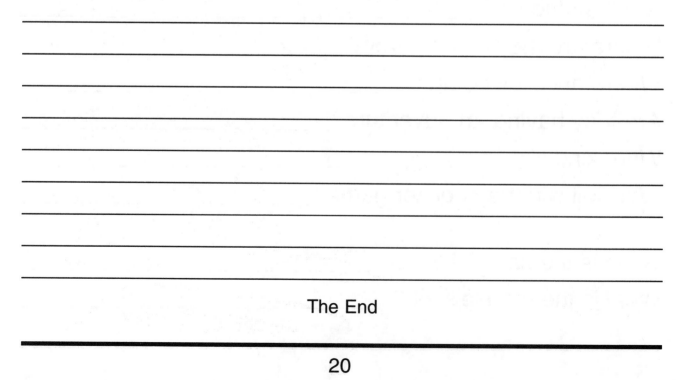

The End

Look closely at the entire picture. Then answer the questions on the next page.

Your answers to these questions will help you write a story about the old woman. Write your answers on the lines.

What is the woman baking? _____

What is she taking out of the oven? _____

What does it smell like? _____

What other smells are in the kitchen?_____

_____

How do the finished cookies taste? _____

_____

Does the old woman like to bake? _____

_____

Who will eat the cakes, cookies, and pies?_____

_____

Does she live alone? _____

Does she have pets?_____

Who are her friends?_____

Is she a witch?_____

If so, is she a good witch or a bad witch?_____

_____

Is she someone's grandma? _____

_____

Use your ideas from the last page to fill in the blanks of this story. After you fill in the blanks, keep writing. YOU decide what happens in the story!

THE OLD LADY IN THE KITCHEN

By _____

Once there was an old lady who loved to bake. She always wore her _____ apron and her _____ hat when she baked. She worked hard in her crowded _____ kitchen. In it were _____, _____, and _____. On the kitchen walls hung _____, _____, and a _____. You could smell the _____, _____, and _____. It always smelled _____ in that kitchen. The cookies always tasted _____! Why did the lady bake so much? Well, she baked all those things because _____

_____

_____

_____

_____

_____

_____

The End

Look closely at the entire picture. Then answer the questions on the next page.

Your answers to these questions will help you write a story about the girl on the swingset. Write your answers on the lines.

What sound does the merry-go-round make? _____

What sound do you hear when the children go down

the slide? _____

What sound does an ice-cream truck make? _____

What sound do you hear when the dog barks? _____

What other sounds do you "hear" in the picture?
List them all.

_____

_____

_____

_____

_____

_____

_____

_____

_____

_____

_____

Use your ideas from the last page to fill in the blanks of this story. You must describe the playground, using only sounds.

SARA GOES TO THE PLAYGROUND

By _____

Sara had an operation to help her see better. Afterward, she had to wear bandages over her eyes. One day her dad said they were going somewhere. "It's a surprise," he said. When Sara got out of the car, the first thing she heard was a _____ sound. "What is that?" she asked. "Listen closely," said her dad. She heard a _____ and a _____. She heard children _____. She heard the _____ of a bat hitting a ball. A dog was _____. A mother was calling "_____." She heard a baby _____. An ice-cream truck bell rang _____. She heard the _____ of a swing. "I know! We're at the park!" Sara said. It was a happy day.

The End

Look closely at both pictures. Then answer the questions below them and on the next page.

Your answers to these questions will help you write letters from the children to each other. Write your answers on the lines.

What are the boy and girl in the snow wearing? _____

_____

What are the boy and girl at the beach wearing? _____

_____

What does snow feel like?_____

What does sand feel like? _____

How are they different? _____

How are they the same? _____

How did all the children's cheeks get red? _____

_____

Is the dog in the snow cold? _____

Is the dog on the beach hot? _____

When the wind blows in the winter, what does it feel like?

_____

When the wind blows in the summer, what does it feel like?

_____

Are the boys and girls having fun? _____

Why do you think so? _____

Use your ideas to fill in the blanks below. The Sandler cousins had never played in snow. The Iceberg cousins had never played on the beach. So one day they traded places! They wrote letters to their cousins, describing what each place felt like! Please complete the letters.

LETTERS TO FIRST COUSINS

By _____

Dear Cousins:

We are at the beach for the first time! It is so _____ here, we do not need coats! The sand feels _____ on our bare feet. It is _____ like snow, but not _____. The sun feels _____. When the tide comes in, it _____ our legs. It feels _____! We like the breezes here, because they feel _____ on our _____ skin. When the sand is dry, it feels _____. When the sand is wet, it is _____, and we make sand castles! The best feeling at the beach is

_____

_____.

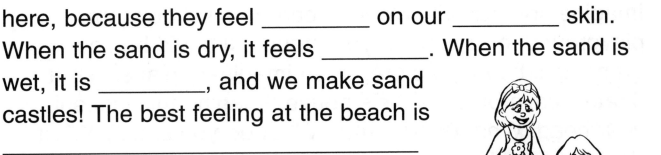

    Your cousins, the Icebergs

Dear Cousins:

We are playing in the snow for the first time! It is _____! All these clothes feel _____ and _____. They keep us _____. The snow is fun! It feels _____ on our skin, so we wear gloves. When the wind blows, our noses _____! We like the feeling of making snowballs. When we get hit with them, it _____! Our dog likes the snow, too. We will make a fire later, and that will feel _____. The best feeling in the snow is when _____

_____.

    Your cousins, the Sandlers

Imagine your favorite place. It can be a schoolroom, a playground, or a room in your house. It could be your grandma's house, a store, or an imaginary place, like a pirate's cave or a dragon's house. Imagine this place in your head. What do you see? What do you smell? What do you hear? Is there anything to taste? Pretend that you can touch the things there. What do they feel like? Write about that place below.

MY SPECIAL PLACE

By_____

Let me tell you about a special place I know. It is _____

_____

_____

_____

_____

_____

_____

_____

_____

_____

_____

_____

_____

_____

The End

Here, draw a picture of the special place you wrote about.

drawn by

Draw a picture of a special person. It could be someone you know, it could be an imaginary person, or it could be YOU! Think about what color hair and eyes that person has. Think about what kind of clothes the person likes to wear. What size is that person? Think about how you want to make that person feel. Is he or she happy or sad? Mad or glad? Scared? What does the person like to do for fun? Does the person work? What kind of job does he or she do?

drawn by _____

Here, describe that special person in a story.

MY SPECIAL PERSON

By _____

Let me tell you about a person I know who is _____

_____

_____

_____

_____

_____

_____

_____

_____

_____

_____

_____

_____

_____

_____

_____

_____

The End

In the next few pages, the beginnings and middles of the stories have been done for you. You have to complete the stories by writing each ending. Don't forget to read them again when you are finished!

A DRAGON IN THE BATHTUB

By _____

Paul was late for school. He ran into the bathroom to brush his teeth and tripped over something. A long, thick green tail was hanging out of the bathtub. Paul pulled the shower curtain back, and there was a dragon! A dragon in the bathtub!

Paul stared at the dragon. The dragon gave him a dirty look.

"Do you mind?" said the dragon. "I'm trying to take a bath!"

Paul had to do something, quick! He

_____

_____

_____

_____

_____

_____

_____

_____

_____

_____

_____

_____

_____

_____

_____

_____

_____

_____

The End

MONKEYS IN AISLE SEVEN

By_____

Mr. Fister the zookeeper was in a panic. Two of his new monkeys were lost somewhere in the neighborhood! Mr. Fister looked all around. He saw a gas station, a beauty parlor, offices, and a big grocery store. Where could the monkeys be?

"Help! Help!" called someone from the grocery store. "There are monkeys in aisle seven! And they're heading for the bananas!"

Mr. Fister ran toward the store. He wondered how much trouble those silly monkeys would get into. When he got there, he found out!

People were running everywhere! A woman with a big hairdo had a jar of peanut butter turned upside down on her head. The store manager was playing pickup sticks with spilled spaghetti. Frozen pizzas were flying through the air like Frisbees! And that was just the beginning!

Next _____

_____

_____

_____

The End

THE TRAPDOOR

By _____

Erik and Liz were bored. It was raining outside, and their parents were spending the day ripping up the old kitchen floor. The children sat in the kitchen, eating apples and watching their parents work. The wooden floor underneath the old one looked old, too! It would have to be polished.

Suddenly, Liz jumped up from her seat. She ran to the middle of the kitchen.

"What's this?" she said, tapping her foot on a square piece of the wooden floor. It sounded hollow!

"It looks like a trapdoor!" said Erik excitedly.

Their dad used a screwdriver to pry it open. It WAS a trapdoor! A staircase went down into the darkness. The children wondered where it led.

Their dad got a flashlight and went in first, followed by their mom. Liz and Erik went next. It was dark and _____

_____

_____

_____

_____

_____

_____

_____

_____

The End

On the next few pages, you will find the beginnings of fairy tales. They might sound different from how you remember them! Finish the stories and create NEW fairy tales that are all your own!

THE THREE BEARS ORDER PIZZA

By _____

Once upon a time there were three bears: Mama Bear, Papa Bear, and Baby Bear. One morning they wanted to eat breakfast, and guess what? There was no porridge!

"What will we do?" cried Papa Bear.

"We will just have to order a pizza," said Mama Bear.

"Hurray!" said Baby Bear. "Pizza for breakfast!"

So the bears ordered a pizza. They waited for it to arrive.

Soon they heard a noise at the front door. But it wasn't the pizza lady! It was _____

_____

_____

_____

_____

_____

_____

The End

JACK AND THE BEAN DIP

By _____

Once there was a little boy named Jack who was very poor. He had to go to the market to sell his cow. On the way, he met an old man who gave him a handful of beans for the cow.

"They are magic beans," the old man said. When Jack got home, he planted the beans. Soon, a stalk grew all the way up to the sky. But Jack didn't think to climb the beanstalk. He just picked the giant beans and made a yummy bean dip from his mother's secret recipe. The bean dip smelled very good. The smell floated up to the sky, where a giant lived.

"FEE, FIE, FO, FUM!" roared the giant. "I smell bean dip, so here I come!" And he started down the _____

_____

_____

_____

_____

_____

_____

_____

_____

The End

SNOW WHITE AND THE SEVEN DRAWERS

By _____

Once there was a princess named Snow White. She was lost in the woods, and she was afraid. Just as it started to get dark, she saw a little house. She looked in the window.

The house was empty except for a tall dresser that stood in the middle of the room. It had seven drawers. Snow White did not know that it was a magic dresser! Each drawer that was opened had a special surprise.

Slowly, Snow White went into the house. She opened the first drawer. All of a sudden _____

_____

_____

_____

_____

_____

_____

_____

_____

_____

_____

_____

_____

_____

_____

_____

_____

_____

_____

_____

_____

The End

Here, you can draw a picture of the ending of your story.

drawn by ✏️ _____

THE THREE BIG PIGS

By _____

Once upon a time there were three big pigs who went out to seek their fortune. When it came time to build a home, the first big pig made his house out of straw. One day, a hungry wolf came to the first big pig's house.

"This looks like a little piggie's house," the wolf said. "I'll huff, and I'll puff, and I'll blow the house down. Then I'll have me a nice ham sandwich!" So the hungry wolf blew the straw house down. There stood the first big pig, and he was mad!

"Wow!" said the hungry wolf. "That pig is BIG!"

The pig _____

_____

_____

_____

_____

_____

_____

_____

_____

_____

_____

_____

_____

_____

_____

_____

_____

_____

_____

The End

Here, you can draw a picture of the ending of your story.

drawn by ✏ _____

On the next few pages, the beginnings and middles of the stories have been done for you. You have to complete the stories by writing each ending. Don't forget to read them again when you are finished!

MY DAY AS A BASKETBALL

By _____

When I woke up this morning, it was like any other school day. I could smell french toast cooking in the kitchen. My pet canary was singing away in the corner. But when I rolled out of bed, I really rolled! I felt . . . round. I bounced over to my mirror to have a look, and guess what I saw? I had been turned into a basketball! What was going to happen to me? I wondered. What would my parents say? What would my teacher say? How would I go to the bathroom?

Suddenly, there was a knock on my door! I _____

_____

_____

_____

_____

_____

_____

_____

_____

_____

_____

_____

_____

_____

_____

The End

Here, you can draw a picture of the ending of your story.

drawn by _____

THERE'S A MONSTER
IN THE GLOVE COMPARTMENT!

By _____

José and Shanah were in the backseat of the car. It had been a long drive. Suddenly, they heard a loud banging noise. They sat up straight and looked around.

"Do you hear that?" they asked their parents.

"No," said their mom and dad.

The children listened carefully. The noise sounded like it was coming from the glove compartment! Their mom reached over to open it. She needed a map.

"Don't do it, Mom!" yelled Shanah, but it was too late. Out popped a

_____

_____

_____

_____

_____

_____

_____

_____

_____

_____

_____

_____

_____

_____

_____

_____

_____

_____

The End

Here, you can draw a picture of the ending of your story.

drawn by _____

The following stories have short beginnings and short endings, but no middles! Read the words given, then write a middle for each story. Read the whole story when you are finished.

ZETI THE ZEBRA LOSES HIS STRIPES

By _____

Zeti the Zebra wanted to go swimming in the river, but his mom said no. Zeti _____

_____

_____

_____

_____

_____

_____

_____

_____

_____

_____

_____

_____

"I hope you learned your lesson, Zeti!" said Mother Zebra.

Zeti shivered under the towel. How he missed his beautiful stripes! He would never disobey his mom again.

The End

A VERY WINDY WALK

By _____

Artie the ant had a problem. He wanted to cross the kitchen floor and get a big, tasty bread crumb. But a giant fan was blowing him backward. He looked around for a way to get across. Artie _____

_____

_____

_____

_____

_____

_____

_____

_____

_____

_____

_____

_____

_____

_____

_____

_____

Artie pulled himself up by the cord and crawled onto the counter. It was a long, hard journey, but he had made it! He munched on the bread crumb while he rested. The trip back would be a breeze!

The End

Read the stories on the following pages. Each story is missing a middle, and each is missing a middle picture. Finish the stories by writing the middles, then draw matching pictures in the space provided. Don't forget to color the pictures!

THE WALKING TREE

By _____

Once there was an unhappy little tree that wanted to walk so badly. One day a fairy princess made its wish come true, and the tree was able to walk. Off the tree went to explore the world!

First it _____

_____

_____

_____

_____

_____

_____

_____

_____

_____

_____

_____

_____

The tree decided to put its roots down in the city. There, it brought shade to all its new friends for years to come. "It's good to be useful again," said the tree happily.

The End

drawn by

THE BARKING CAT

By _____

One sunny day, Doogie the dog was chasing Kitty the cat around the yard. "I wish I were a dog," said Kitty, breathing hard. "I would _____

_____

_____

_____

_____

_____

_____

_____

_____

_____

_____

_____

_____

_____

Kitty was glad to be a cat again. Now, if only she could get Doogie to come out of the tree!

The End

drawn by ✏ _____

WRAPUNZEL

By _____

Once there was a beautiful young girl named Wrapunzel who had been put in a high tower by a wicked witch. The witch made poor, lonely Wrapunzel wrap presents all day and night! She wasn't allowed to see anybody. Each night, when she went to bed, Wrapunzel _____

_____

_____

_____

_____

_____

_____

_____

_____

_____

_____

But the wicked witch's tall hat got caught in the elevator door. And that was the end of the wicked witch. Since the elevator had been put in, Wrapunzel's friends could visit any time they wanted. So Wrapunzel decided to stay in the tower, and she lived there happily ever after.

The End

drawn by _____

A ROCKING, ROLLING ROAD TRIP

By _____

Once upon a time there were three large rocks sitting around in the dirt. The rocks were all feeling bored.

"How come we never get to go anywhere or do anything?" said a rock named Hal. "I want to _____

_____

_____

_____

_____

_____

_____

_____

_____

_____

_____

_____

_____

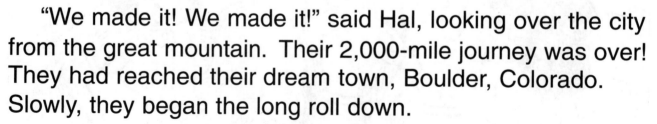

"We made it! We made it!" said Hal, looking over the city from the great mountain. Their 2,000-mile journey was over! They had reached their dream town, Boulder, Colorado. Slowly, they began the long roll down.

The End

drawn by _____

For the next two exercises, look at the pictures. Write a story to go with each picture. Don't just describe the pictures. Tell stories about what you think is going on. Think about what happened before, or after. There are no right or wrong stories, just YOUR stories! When you're done, give your story a title.

_____

By _____

_____

_____

_____

_____

The End

_____

By _____

_____

_____

_____

_____

_____

_____

_____

_____

_____

The End

What if there were a town where everyone walked backward? How would the cars be designed? The roads? Would people have eyes in the back of their heads, or mirrors on their hats? Which way would their shoes face? Think about Backward Town. Write your ideas on the lines below. You can tell a story, or just make a list of ideas for a story you may write later.

BACKWARD TOWN

By _____

_____

_____

_____

_____

_____

_____

_____

_____

_____

_____

_____

_____

The End

What if you woke up one morning and you were an old man or woman? How would your day be different? How would it be the same? What games would you play with your friends? Would you do better in school? What would you do differently? What would be fun about being old? What would not be so good? Describe what you would look like and what you would wear. Write your ideas on the lines below. You can tell a story, or just make a list of ideas for a story you may write later.

WHEN I'M OLD

By _____

_____

_____

_____

_____

_____

_____

_____

_____

_____

_____

_____

_____

_____

_____

_____

_____

_____

_____

_____

_____

_____

_____

_____

The End

Here, you can draw a picture to go with your story.

drawn by _____

What if you could step into a time machine and go anywhere, backward or forward in time? Where would you go? Would you go back to the time of the dinosaurs? What would you do there? What would your job be? How about the time of the cowboys? What about going into the future? Can you imagine living on a different planet, or in a spaceship? Use your imagination! You can go anywhere and do anything! Write your ideas on the lines below. You can tell a story, or just make a list of ideas for a story you may write later.

TIME TRAVEL

By _____

_____

_____

_____

_____

_____

_____

_____

_____

_____

_____

_____

_____

_____

_____

_____

_____

_____

_____

_____

_____

_____

The End

Here, you can draw a picture to go with your story.

drawn by ✎ _____

What if you were in your bedroom, but you were a tiny bug, crawling on the floor? What would everything look like? What would your shoes look like? Your dolls? Your baseball? Your clothes? To a bug, your everyday items would look very, very different! If you want, work on this page in your room. Lie on the floor and pretend that you are the same size as a bug! Write your ideas on the lines below. You can tell a story, or just make a list of ideas for a story you may write later.

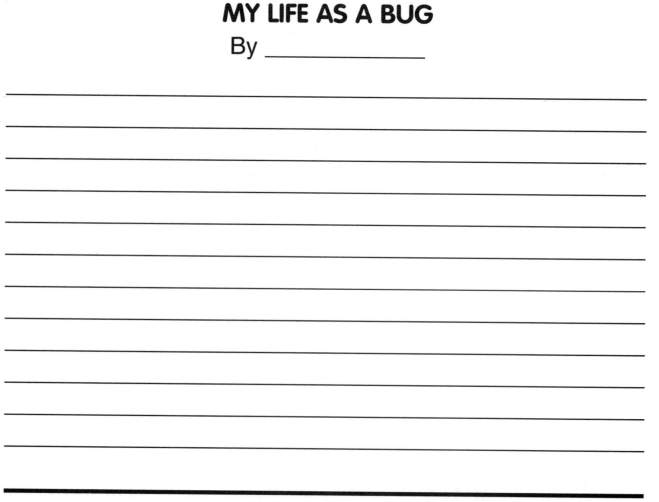

MY LIFE AS A BUG

By _____

_____

_____

_____

_____

_____

_____

_____

_____

_____

_____

_____

_____

_____

_____

_____

_____

_____

_____

_____

_____

_____

_____

_____

The End

Here, you can draw a picture to go with your story.

drawn by ✏️ _____

Read the words listed below. They are very different! Your job is to write a story using ALL of these words. They can play a big part in your story, or just get a quick mention. But all five words must be found somewhere in the story. Have fun! When you're done, give your story a title.

HOUSE   BROWN   PILOT   EGG   BICYCLE

By _____

_____

_____

_____

_____

_____

_____

_____

_____

_____

_____

_____

_____

_____

_____

The End

Read the words listed below. They are very different! Your job is to write a story using ALL of these words. They can play a big part in your story, or just get a quick mention. But all the words must be found somewhere in the story. Have fun! When you're done, give your story a title.

SCIENTIST DOG BONE CHEESE PAPER CLIP CHEWY

_____

By _____

_____
_____
_____
_____
_____
_____
_____
_____
_____
_____
_____
_____
_____
_____

Advanced Exercise/Use All the Words

The End

On the lines below, write all about yourself. This is called an author biography, and you are the author of this book! You can include your age, what you look like, where you live, and what you like to do. In the space provided, you can paste a picture of yourself, or draw a self-portrait.

ABOUT THE AUTHOR